When I Return, I'm Coming Back As My Poodle

How to Feel Loved and Adored Even if You Don't Feel Loved and Adored

Pamela Simmons

Copyright © 2017 Pamela Simmons.
All rights reserved. No portion of this book may be reproduced mechanically, electronically, or by any other means, including photocopying, without written permission of the publisher. It is illegal to copy this book, post it to a website, or distribute it by any other means without permission from the publisher.

Published by Pamela Simmons
www.pamelasimmonscounseling.com
pamela@pamelasimmonscounseling.com

LIMITS OF LIABILITY AND DISCLAIMER OF WARRANTY

The author/publisher shall not be liable for your misuse of this material. This book is strictly for informational and educational purposes.

WARNING & DISCLAIMER

The purpose of this book is to educate and entertain. It is distributed with the understanding that the publisher is not engaged in the dispensation of legal, psychological or any other professional advice. The content of each entry is the expression and opinion of its author and does not necessarily reflect the beliefs, practices or viewpoints of the publisher, its parent company or its affiliates. The publisher's choice to include any material within is not intended to express or imply any warranties or guarantees of any kind. The author and/or publisher do not guarantee that anyone following these techniques, suggestions, tips, ideas, or strategies will become successful. The author and/or publisher shall have neither liability nor responsibility to anyone with respect to any loss or damage caused, or alleged to be caused, directly or indirectly by the information contained in this book.

ISBN-13:978-1979337144
ISBN-10:1979337144

ABOUT THE AUTHOR

Pamela Simmons is a licensed professional counselor and supervisor of counselor interns in Texas. She has tried on many hats. She has been a church program director, a camp counselor and recreation leader, a sales clerk, a math teacher, a math tutor, and now a counselor. She has had a column in three local papers with more articles than she can count. She presents on Authentic Happiness and Building Lives of Joy.

As a writer, columnist, teacher, counselor, coach, workshop and seminar leader, she enhances her work with humor and humanness. She guides you toward the love and joy you are designed to have in your life. Her life and executive coaching program is a respected and recognized one for participants who would like to meet by phone from anywhere in the United States.

www.joyfulrelationship.us

DEDICATED TO THOSE WHO
HUNGER TO FEEL LOVED

Contents

11	Chapter 1
13	Chapter 2
17	Chapter 3
19	Chapter 4
23	Chapter 5
25	Chapter 6
29	Chapter 7
31	Chapter 8
35	Chapter 9
37	Chapter 10
39	Chapter 11
43	Chapter 12
45	Chapter 13
47	Chapter 14
51	Chapter 15
59	Life and Loving and Teachings
81	Epilogue
85	About the Author
86	Acknowledgments

When I return, I want to be my poodle. Loved adoringly no matter what I do. I look at my little guy, and there's nothing he can do wrong. No criticism—just love and adoration. And the same for his sister, Sophie. She can do anything, and I will love her and adore her forever. My parents may have felt that way, but never told me. I do remember Mom saying things like, "I'm 'usually' so proud of you."

Chapter 1

My dad was in the Army, so moving was inevitable. I was born in Heidelberg, Germany; went to kindergarten in Alaska, elementary school in Illinois and Indiana; two junior highs in North Carolina; and high school in Arkansas. That's six schools in eighteen years. I have met people who attended twelve schools in twelve years, so I am grateful for some consistency.

Although moving around has its pluses, it can also be disorienting. About the time I made friends, it was time to move again. If things weren't going well with those friends, it was a relief. With other friends it was a loss.

Kindergarten in Alaska brought fun in the form of building an igloo I could actually sit inside; and playing with kids in the neighborhood. It also brought despair with my brother getting meningitis and changing our lives forever. He was 3 years old; I was 5 years old.

Meningitis is a disease that affects the brain and spinal cord. Its symptoms can be flulike and lead parents to treat it as such. If not diagnosed quickly enough, brain damage occurs.

In our case, my brother lost hearing in his left ear and had some brain damage. He disrupted activities at home and in his classroom at school. He slept on his good ear, making it next to impossible to arouse him in the morning. I would have loved that option during the years his music blasted us or when I slept under the parents' bedroom. Mom would say, "I think he had some brain damage."

In Alaska, when Dad came home from work, he frolicked with the two of us for a few minutes, and then sent us to the basement to play. He and Mom stayed in the living room drinking and talking. Playing with Alan was like playing with a scorpion. I never knew when he would strike. He would be quiet, and out of nowhere I would feel the sting: pulling my ears, chasing me, pinching me. I so longed to be upstairs talking with my parents. Dad did not intervene, and when Mom did, Alan would get her to laugh. I was miserable around him. I loved him, but hated how he treated me. He was 3 years old then. My sister was born right after his diagnosis, and right before we moved again.

A family member's bad health can greatly affect the time and energy parents have for all the children. The same is true when a death occurs. A loss of a parent or child or other family member requires grieving time that takes away from the time children need for care and development. How children interpret these changes can affect how they perceive themselves and how loved they feel.

Chapter 2

We moved to Fort Sheridan in Illinois for my first through sixth grade years, with an intervening year in Indiana for third grade. Dad travelled a lot due to his job as an Army pilot, many times flying the General to Army bases in other parts of the country.

We lived in Army housing with rows of two story apartments arranged in an open rectangle with a huge greenbelt where we played and rode bikes. In the early days, Mom read us bedtime stories. We were all in our pajamas propped up with pillows on her big bed, as she read selections from Curious George before putting us in our own beds. I loved those moments—all of us cuddled together, soothed by the warmth of her voice and an arm around us.

I was six years old and listened to Dick Biondi, The Wild I-Tralian—yes, THE WILD I-TRALIAN—on WLS Chicago every day as he played Elvis Presley, Jerry Lee Lewis, Pat Boone, and Perry Como. Biondi was one of the original "screamers" known for his shouting delivery as well as his wild antics on the air and off. His fits of temper and jokes gone wrong kept listeners captivated. He used to say he had been fired twenty-three times. A song he wrote and made popular was "On Top of a Pizza" sung to the tune of "On Top of Old Smokey."

> On top of a pizza, all covered with cheese
> I met my first meat ball when somebody sneezed
> It fell off the table and on to the floor
> Then rolled and rolled, right out of the door.

The hula hoop came out about that time too. In our living room near our Sears Roebuck white sofa, table, and two French provincial chairs, my brother and I twirled the hula hoop to the sound of Jim Lowe singing "Green Door," Elvis' "Don't Be Cruel," or "Hot Diggity Doggity" by Perry Como, "Be-Bop-a-lula" by Gene Vincent, or Gale Storm's "Why Do Fools Fall in Love." Mom laughed as she watched us. Other times we took the hula hoop outside so the other kids in the neighborhood could do it with us, or we had a contest to see who could keep it going the longest. Another contest came much later at a work event in the 1980s, where one hundred sales people donned fifties poodle skirts and saddle oxfords while twirling their hoops. I was among those who kept the hoop going the longest.

When my brother first learned to ride his bike, he rode around and around the greenbelt area pedaling as fast as he could. Then he jumped off the bike, and watched it crash into my friend Marie Hagedorn's porch. God, he was painful to watch. I, of course, rode cautiously around the greenbelt, slowly applied the brake, and stopped.

I loved Ft. Sheridan with ravines and the lake and lots of kids around. The very best year ever was fifth grade with Mr. Dropp. We had spelling bees and state capital competition. We played a lot of softball together as a class; or swung on the hanging bars; or played Red Rover. We laughed all day in his class while learning tons about math, climate, literature, and science.

Mr. Dropp became a hero the first day of school. He took attendance and then dismissed us. Every day after that was an adventure in his class. He read aloud *The Time Machine* and The Raven; we played chess one hour each week; he gave us Hero Medals for accomplishments; and he brought his motorcycle mechanic Spider Webb to class one day.

Elaine in the front row interrupted frequently with, "Mr. Dropp, why do we have to learn this?" "So you will do better than Mary Margaret McGoon or Natalie Attired," he quipped. These are two characters from the famous radio duo Bob and Ray from WLS 89AM

Chapter 2

in Chicago. Bob and Ray spoofs and parodies kept drivers awake to and from work every day, and Mr. Dropp took advantage of every opportunity to quote them. Phil in the back row had to explain the wisecracks Mr. Dropp made to the students around him, and spent many hours after school writing "I will not talk in class" five hundred times. Phil and Mr. Dropp were Bob and Ray for our class.

Our school was a mix of the many Jewish students in Highland Park, some Italian Catholics from Highwood, and the Army children from Ft. Sheridan, many of whom rode the Army bus to school with Mr. Day, our driver.

Years ago, I made contact with Phil through Classmates.com. He arranged a phone conversation with Mr. Dropp who joyfully said he loved all his "pretty girls" and missed teaching. I reminded him about the day my mother let me wear my grandmother's wedding ring to school. I naively put it on my left ring finger. Mr. Dropp got on one knee next to my desk, took my hand, and said, "Will you marry me?" My face turned beet red and my mouth could not speak. As the class laughed hysterically, I was embarrassed, and also enamored.

A disabling motor cycle accident put a halt to his teaching not long after our class started junior high. Since many of my school photos were lost over the years, Phil sent me a copy of his. I love looking at that picture.

Positive school moments make a huge difference to a young girl living with a scorpion.

Chapter 3

In the background of these experiences, my parents drank a lot. Cocktails every evening. I wasn't aware of the drunkenness until one night I woke up and saw my dad stumbling in the hallway. There are very few things more distressing than realizing the dad you adore is drunk.

Fortunately he could not drink the night before a flight, so that helped while he was in the service. That didn't change Mom's drinking habits. She didn't work or have to fly a plane. But it would have helped to have her sober after five p.m. to read books to us again. I really missed the few moments of peace with Mom and the scorpion, who while reading those books, was calm.

I had a lot of leg aches from eight to ten years old. Mom came to my room in the middle of the night when I woke from pain and rubbed them until I fell back to sleep. How comforting it was to feel the warmth of her hands soothe the pain in my legs. She did many loving and helpful things, among the not so helpful things.

She made costumes for the school play and made sure I was dressed well for any occasion according to her standards.

"No daughter of mine is wearing that outfit!"

I heard those words when I wanted a Dale Evans outfit, when I wanted a Shirley Temple haircut, and when I wanted this awesome quilted skirt with an elastic waistband my best friend Nancy had. She didn't mind when Nancy and I did a duet from *My Fair Lady* for the school talent show in sixth grade, but for mom curly hair and cowgirls were not okay.

Shirley Temple and Dale Evans were role models in the 1950's and not bad ones either. But my mom wanted to be sure I looked the way she wanted. Back then I wanted to be a hero too. My brother just wanted to be one of the Three Stooges. He mimicked them at every opportunity, flicking his chin or mine, and pulling ears, and slapping. He annoyed me beyond toleration with their slapstick shenanigans and stupid noises like eh eh eh.

We had dinner together at the table every night except Sunday, when we had chicken in a basket in the basement watching Ed Sullivan and *Gunsmoke* on the new color TV. Dad changed the basement to a TV room by building a case for the TV in the corner, so we all watched together. That was probably the first built in TV armoire. We also celebrated birthdays at the dining table with our favorite meals. Mine was spaghetti. I'll never forget when I got a record player and a 45 rpm record of "Mack the Knife" on one side and "Beyond the Sea" on the other. I really miss Bobby Darren.

Mom took me to Sunday school every Sunday and to choir practice, and found a children's Bible for me. I wanted to say "got me a children's Bible"—but my sixth grade honors English teacher said to never use get or got in good writing. I don't think I have used those words since—except right here. Mom's friend Jean Schramm started a Brownie Troop where we learned to make a bed with square corners, sell Girl Scout cookies door to door, and went on campouts and cooked on a tin can. Mom and Jean also started a nursery service that kept kids entertained and supervised while the adults went out on Saturday nights. One of my fondest memories is my dad picking me up from the little cot I fell asleep on at the nursery, and carrying me to the car to take home.

Chapter 4

It was in 6th grade honors English that Nancy Nicholson and I became good friends. Nancy was a kind, smart, thin only child with wispy blond hair and a high forehead covered with thin bangs. Her mother was tall and had thin light brown hair cut in a pageboy and bangs. I wanted bangs too, but Mom said, "Why do you want those insipid bangs?"

Nancy's house had hardwood floors with area rugs from the orient. She was her parents' only child, so when visiting her home, her parents were engaging. One nice summer evening on their back patio, they grilled hamburgers with sliced avocados for appetizers. It was the first taste of avocados I ever experienced. They tasted so good, I had to resist the temptation to put my face on the plate and devour it all. While waiting for dinner, Nancy and I jumped rope singing, "Who's got short shorts? I've got short shorts." Once everything was prepared, we dined and talked together. I don't recall the conversation, but I do recall how lovely it was to have a dinner and conversation during which even I was able to speak. Unlike dining with my brother who interrupted every sentence, there was a nice flow to the table talk.

Nancy was a rule follower like I was and use to write stories about Sweet Little Lydia, a precocious and adventuresome little girl. Nancy didn't have a scorpion in her life. Sometimes Lydia took the Tiny Tears doll from her best friend and made her guess where it was. Later they would find it in the forest sitting on a rock overlooking the water.

Sometimes she escaped her mother's watchful eyes and snuck down to the ravine to meet with friends and collect frogs and turtles, returning home proudly with her catch. Her horrified mother would yell, "Lydia, what have you gotten into now!" One time Lydia snuck up quietly behind her mom and popped a balloon. Her mom peed in her pants she was so frightened. Lydia sounds a bit like Scorpion, doesn't she?

Nancy's dad was a lieutenant colonel, so her family lived in red brick housing near us. We spent hours together swimming, playing, writing, and even singing. We made a large wooden floor plan for our dolls to play on; we did every version of jump rope we could find or make up; and we swam at the Navy Base pool or Lake Michigan often.

For the spring talent show, we performed a duet to "All I Want Is a Room Somewhere" from *My Fair Lady*. Dressed in rags and the fingerless gloves of Eliza Doolittle, we sang exuberantly. I don't recall my mother being in the audience at that talent show.

When I was in first grade, I attended one ballet class, and then was put in the class show. When Mom and I returned from the show, she said to me, "When you dance, you are not supposed to look at your feet." I felt shame. I now feel anger, since one dance class is hardly enough to prepare a six-year-old for a performance. She never entered me in another dance class.

It was also in sixth grade that I was taller than Nancy or other friends, so unconsciously I must have bent over to make eye contact. Mom said, "Don't slouch! Get a book and walk up and down the stairs without it falling off your head. Do this ten times." She also poked me in the back so I would remember to stand up tall. I was so glad when we moved to Little Rock where I had a friend who was five inches taller. I hung out with her a lot.

I was such a rule follower—military family and first child wasn't about to break a rule. When my mother told me to keep my legs together when I started dating, I did. No sex until the week before

Chapter 4

my wedding and even felt guilty about that. I didn't realize a lot of my friends were having sex and some of them with my boyfriends.

In the summer, parents joined the neighbors in the backyard drinking whiskey sours. We were usually playing outside with our friends until dark. In the winter, parents had a cocktail in the living room, and then we all spent some time watching TV in the basement, until we went to bed around 8:00.

Mom always had music going during the day. Albums from *My Fair Lady*, *Camelot*, *South Pacific*, *Carousel*, filled the house with melodies I still sing today. I recall going to a high school production of *Carousel* with a friend and her family. I fell in love with the lead male, Billy Bigelow, a charming roguish barker for the carousel. All these musicals had handsome male lead characters and beautiful female lead characters. I sang every song with the album and pretended to be part of the play, and carried away by my handsome gentleman, who loved and adored me.

The music was an escape from Scorpion's haunting reputation. His antics increased in intensity and legality. Several times he stole things from the Base Exchange, and took my five-year-old sister with him to teach her how to do it too. When Mom found the things he stole, she took him and the item to the Exchange and had him apologize. Dad never did a thing.

It was the summer after sixth grade when all the kids gathered in the greenbelt to play baseball or bounce or fly. Buddy lived just across the greenbelt from me and we developed a crush on each other. One day he asked me to go see a Jerry Lewis movie playing at the base. I remember Mom dressing me in a lavender gingham dress and matching shoes for the occasion. Buddy knocked on our front door and the two of us began our one-mile walk to the base movie theater. We could walk or ride bikes to the library, the lake, the Base Exchange, the tennis courts, and the movie theater. I did not say one word all the way to the theater. The movie was *Cinderfella* and very funny, so we enjoyed laughing at Jerry Lewis. On the way back home, I might have said a few words, but not many. He tried making conversation. It had to be exhausting for him.

A few weeks later, I learned that Buddy would be moving away. That happened a lot on Army bases. Families moved in and moved out. I was sitting in the shade under a tree talking with a friend and crying a little because Buddy was moving. Mom stuck her head out the door and said, "You have a mother, you know!" I was shocked and didn't know what to think. She was a master of head-scratching comments. Her mother died when she was eighteen years old, so she had issues. In sixth grade I had no idea what to make of it.

When I was an adult and visiting Mom one weekend, she said to me, "I had three diaphragm babies." What a lovely thing to tell me. I said, "Well, Mom, you have to put the thing in for it to work." Did this mean she never wanted any of us? Did this mean she was too sexually driven to decide ahead of time what to do to avoid pregnancy? I just shook my head and went to play tennis with a friend.

Chapter 5

My dad had to go back to Germany at the beginning of my seventh grade year. So he decided the rest of us would move in with his mother in Rocky Mount, NC, from 1961–1963. He actually paid for his mother's house, because his son Flake lived with Mama and Papa—Dad's parents. See, my dad had a child out of wedlock before he met Mom. While Dad was away in the Army, Mama and Papa took care of little Flake and Dad sent money regularly to support them. When my parents married, they wanted to take Flake with them, but Mama and Papa wouldn't have it. The unfortunate thing for Flake was that Mama and Papa expected him to do nothing, so he did what they expected. Papa died in 1959, so when we moved in with Mama, Flake was away in the service; so the little house could accommodate all of us.

Those two years with Mama taught me how it was that my dad didn't know how to love. Poor guy didn't have a chance. His parents were like stone. Papa had died two years before. Through the infrequent visits we had with them, he didn't say much. They never came to visit us. Dad would arrange to take an Army plane and fly us down to visit them every now and then. I had air sickness and spent most of the plane time vomiting or sleeping.

Mama rose early every day to put on a pot of collard greens, chicken and dumplings, fry some corn bread, and make homemade biscuits. This was the ritual conducted when Papa was still alive. Supper is served in the evening in Rocky Mount; dinner at noon. So, the early morning ritual was to prepare for the big meal at noon.

When I returned from school each day, Mama was watching *As the World Turns*. There was no hug followed by "Hi honey, how was your day? Would you like a cookie?" Instead, she kept watching her soaps in her chair, not moving until time to heat up the food she started in the morning. She didn't talk except to or about the characters in *All My Children*, frowning as she disapproved of them. I always wondered how she felt about me. As we piled in the car the day we left for Little Rock, she wept.

Chapter 6

My mother would say you could spit from one side of Rocky Mount to the other. Even so, Rocky Mount is in two counties, Nash and Edgemont. When we moved there, my sister's walk to school was half a block. It was the same elementary school my dad attended.

My seventh grade year was at Parker Junior High in Nash County. Mom drove me to school in the morning, then I walked forty-five minutes home, crossed the railroad tracks separating Nash and Edgemont counties, and stopped at Belk Tyler's where Mom worked. Mom loved fashion and usually found jobs in stores with great clothes.

Belk Tyler in Rocky Mount was a two-story department store with fashionable clothes and shoes. I had not been in any department stores in Ft. Sheridan except the Base Exchange, so I found it intriguing. As I entered, there were counters everywhere, and a path to an escalator leading to the second floor. I found Mom and Mrs. Whitley visiting as they waited on customers. The sales people would ooh and ah over how much my mother and I looked alike. Mom would smile with delight. I smiled too, but was not quite certain why. Mom was pretty. I wasn't so sure I was.

I learned early on not to disagree with adults. One day while still at Ft. Sheridan, Mom was sharing a story with a friend of hers. I corrected something she said to which she admonished me with a scowl and a sneer, "If I say black is white, you better leave it that way!" One time my sister sat at a formal dinner party with my parents and two other couples. When everyone had an empty plate, Mom asked, "Would anyone care for seconds?" My sister said, "I would." Mom slapped her on the cheek in front of everyone.

Mom outfitted me quite well with clothes she bought at Belk Tyler. I recall a white and denim blue striped shift she had monogrammed in red with my initials. Mom LOVED monograms and almost everything she owned had a monogram on it. I could wear the sleeveless shift with or without a blouse. I really liked that dress, but when I wore it without a blouse, the girls in Rocky Mount were aghast. Their comments like, "You don't have on a blouse!" were embarrassing. My arm pits started sweating and my face turned bright red. Another of my favorites was a camel hair shift with an A-line skirt. It looked great with a nice belt and my Wejuns. Wejuns were the loafers of the time that you could buy in burgundy leather or navy blue. My navy blue Wejuns had a tassel and I loved them even though they were just a wee bit smaller than my toes needed. Walking forty-five minutes home was a little challenging in them, but it was worth it to gaze at the tassel and smile at how good they looked.

Mom's friend Mrs. Whitley had two teen daughters and turned out to be a great resource for her since she knew a lot about activities available for my age group. I continued my walk home from Belk Tyler, passing an area where black people congregated in the afternoon. I was never afraid, since I had black friends at Ft. Sheridan; but Mom educated me about the 1960s attitude toward black people in the south. Then I passed a Hardee's a few blocks from the house and bought a Pepsi for ten cents. They drink Pepsi in Rocky Mount. They also had this funny drink called Dr. Pepper which I grew to like quite well. They had Coca Cola in Ft. Sheridan.

Behind Mama's little red brick house was a cotton mill. Rocky Mount was founded around a cotton mill built at the falls of the Tar River. That mill sustained the city until the 1990s when it closed. Living behind a cotton mill meant that cotton seed oil hung in the

Chapter 6

air and on clothes and window screens and grass much of the year. Its nutty aroma was pleasant. My bedroom window in the back of the house faced the mill. We had an attic fan to cool the upstairs and warm breezes from the fan kept us comfortable.

Many of my dad's relatives either worked in the mill, or the railroad, or were police officers. The mill provided housing and benefits for the workers and the area around Mama's house is now an historic area, since the mill closed.

Mama's sister was Aunt Annie. She and Uncle Ramsey lived about a mile from Mama's house. One evening Aunt Annie and Uncle Ramsey had us all over for supper—Mama, Mom, Scorpion, my sister, and me. They had a daughter Betty who had a baby daughter named Jane who lived there too.

They lived in a small frame house with no air conditioning and tired worn wooden floors in the entry and small living room. From there we entered a small kitchen with linoleum floors and a big potbellied stove and a long table to accommodate everyone. The gingham curtains swayed from the warm breeze coming through the open window. The aroma of yummy fried chicken filled the room, and with it came potato salad, fresh green beans, newly made delicious sweet iced tea; a meal to savor. They all spoke with a long Southern drawl that was hard to understand for my Chicago bred ears. After supper we would all go to the front porch where we waved at neighbors walking by. It was pleasant hanging out with them on the front porch. Nobody was drinking, and conversation included the children as well as the adults. Uncle Ramsey's pipe smoking ritual mesmerized me: slowly and carefully fill the pipe with tobacco, stuff and pack the tobacco, light the pipe, take a big inhale puffing out little whiffs of smoke to start the pipe. All of this done as he spoke a word or two between puffs, and eventually finished his tale about the long hours at the mill with no break and low pay, and the status of extended family I had not yet met.

Chapter 7

Seventh grade was uneventful, but when I went to Edwards Junior High for eighth grade, it was a five-minute drive or a twenty-minute walk to school. Eighth grade is where I met so many new friends and I felt welcomed and embraced. My algebra teacher convinced me to run for treasurer of the class. I had no idea how to run for an office, so she suggested I find a campaign manager and make posters. Priscilla sat in front of me in algebra, so I asked her to do the job. She sort of accepted and put some effort into it. I had no idea who to turn to for help, though I asked Mom and she said to make posters. Theresa Rhodes was also running for treasurer and evidently really worried I would beat her. She had tons of posters and already knew lots of people. I cannot even remember what I said at my speech, but I do remember when they announced the winner and Theresa was sitting right next to me. She won, and I felt relief, since I also did not know how to be a treasurer.

Chapter 8

Soon after we arrived in Rocky Mount, Papa's sister Eleanor, a hair dresser, welcomed us with open arms; gave us all haircuts; and invited us over to her house to make pizzas and go to the high school Friday night football game. Eleanor had a son Russell Junior her oldest, a daughter Barbara who was three years older than me, and a son Donnie who was my age: thirteen years old. Eleanor's husband Russell Senior spent a lot of time napping on the sofa and watching TV. I learned later he was an alcoholic. I don't recall him ever getting up to greet us when we came to visit. I learned this year that he eventually stopped drinking after many conversations with, and respect shown from, a local pastor.

This particular evening was my first introduction to the phenomena of high school football in the South.

It was a beautiful evening with fans shouting at the teams and people wandering back and forth for food and beverages and a good place to sit or stand. I didn't know anything about the game, but was intrigued by the high energy and enthusiasm.

1961–1963 in Rocky Mount was the time of Chubby Checker and the Twist making its way to households across America. One evening our Aunt Eleanor and Donnie came over for hamburgers.

Mama's living room was small with one very floral sofa, two wing back chairs, and a small TV by the small fire place. One of the four windows with white curtains held an air conditioning unit. How all seven of us fit in the room, I don't know. An arched doorway took us to the dining room with a table for eight and my favorite piece of furniture—an antique mirrored coat rack. One could barely make it to the kitchen from the dining room due to all the furniture, but the table did accommodate us all for dinner.

Donnie, a tall lanky teen, ate his hamburger before I had finished mine. We all watched with amusement as he asked for the next hamburger, and then another, and another and another. He slowly and carefully chewed every bite of all six hamburgers. None of us had ever witnessed more than two hamburgers eaten at a time. After the hamburger feast, we put on a Chubby Checker record and did the twist. Mom brought out some towels used to create the movement of the twist by pretending to dry your body after a bath. We laughed a lot as we all tried to do it awkwardly—my six-year-old sister, Scorpion, Eleanor, Donnie, Mom and me. Mama watched with amusement, shock, and a little of that judgmental frown she has when watching *Days of Our Lives*. Baptists back then didn't dance.

Rocky Mount was a cultural shock in many ways. First, my name in Ft. Sheridan, just north of Chicago was Pam pronounced with a short A as in Apple or At. In Rocky Mount my name became two syllables: PAH-YUM. In my first class math, my teacher called my name, but I didn't answer since it wasn't my name. She called my name as PAH-YUM several times until I realized that since she was looking at me, perhaps she was indeed calling on me. My face turned bright red as I stumblingly replied to her question.

The second cultural shock was the attitude toward black people. My black friends lived on the Army base with the rest of us, so I didn't understand that there were black areas of town and white areas, and black schools and white schools, and black bathrooms and white bathrooms, and white drinking fountains and black drinking fountains, white areas of the bus and black areas of the bus.

In revisiting the culture of Rocky Mount in 1961–1963, I learned that North Carolina had the highest number of KKK members in

Chapter 8

the U.S. It makes me wonder how many of my friends' family members were involved. It has always been difficult to understand the divisiveness. It's also embarrassing to recall all the derogatory names my dad had for every different culture in the U.S. Having lived in his mother's home for two years, it's easier to have compassion for him but I still find it confusing that my mother could tolerate his attitude. My mother was kind to everyone she encountered. I am grateful and appreciative of her respect of all people. My poor dad was always kind to anyone he met, or anyone who came to the door. As soon as the door closed, his tirade of racial slurs flew like bullets on a battle field.

In spite of things being chaotic at home in NC, I made some great friends. Girls asked me to hang out with them. That usually included walking around town talking loudly from one friend's house to another in our culottes and bobby socks and Wejuns. I was impressed with some of the nicer homes my friends had. Ours had cardboard walls upstairs, tastefully decorated with yellow flowered wallpaper. There were things happening all the time in eighth grade, and I loved it. Basketball games, pranks in the lunch room including our table trying to eat all the donuts, so the next lunch wouldn't have any. Changing classes and saying "hey" to people we passed in the hallway. "Hey" is what they say in North Carolina instead of "hi." A popular ninth grader had a crush on me, and we got together a few times. I still had a yearning for the Billy Bigelo boy I met last summer at the pool, so my relationship with the ninth grader didn't last. My friends thought I was crazy and got mad at me after that. I could tell because they stopped saving me a seat in art class.

When I came home from hanging with my friends one day, I was preparing a bath. Mama had venetian blinds in the downstairs bathroom—the one tub in the house. My brother had figured out that he could see through the blinds even when closed, so he invited a guy from down the street to join him watching me. I heard noises outside the window and it scared me and I screamed and cried. Mom came to the door and asked what was wrong. I said some people were watching me from outside. She called the police, but they couldn't find anything. Scorpion strikes again. I knew it was him. Mom probably knew it was him. Nobody could prove anything.

Chapter 9

Toward the latter part of eighth grade my dad returned from Germany. Mom drove to New York to pick him up and bring him home; probably so they would have some time to themselves before entering a house full of kids and Mama.

The Easter Sunday after he returned, we all went to church in our Easter finery: suits for Dad and Scorpion, matching dresses for my mom, my sister, and me. After church, we stepped out of the car and walked the ten paces to the house to have Easter dinner (lunch) with Mama. Dad walked behind me and said to me, "Pam, stand up straight."

Just recently I was in my current home in the bathroom where the walls were opened to find a mystery leak. As I gazed at the wooden posts supporting the walls, I floated back to Rocky Mount and our little house, and I saw the upstairs bathroom with card board walls, the unfinished shower stall with cardboard walls. This was the shower where Scorpion would make a peephole to watch me dress. No matter how many times I plugged the peephole, he would just make another. Our family was like that—peeping at each other and tiptoeing around watching and hoping for someone to say, "I love you" or "Tell me about your day." Empty of love because neither of my parents had love to give. They were stoic and good workers, but untouchable. I hungered to be touched and appreciated. In the two years Dad was in Germany, he never once called us kids, or sent a letter to any of us.

Dad, who retired from the Army upon returning from Germany, tried getting work. He worked with a realtor for a while, but Mom found out this realtor was a bit unscrupulous, and encouraged Dad to do something else. He tried and couldn't find anything that required his skillset, so they decided we should move to Little Rock where Mom grew up. Dad went to Little Rock first, since we were still in school, and we followed once summer came.

My boyfriend that summer was Gordon, and my closest friend was Nina—the youngest daughter of nine children. I hung out with her in the summer while her parents ran a grocery store during the day. She and I would do her chores and then walk around. Nina gave me a good-bye party, during which Gordon kissed me while dancing to "It's My Party, and I'll Cry if I Want To." I hadn't been kissed since Dennis kissed me on the bus in first grade. It was nice to feel special and have a good-bye party and a kiss.

Chapter 10

There were a couple of girls near our new house with real walls in Little Rock, but in spite of my efforts to get together with them, it was rare. Then ninth grade started, and I had a wonderful year. Some fun girls befriended me, so weekends were busy hanging out with them. A handsome guy, Tim, in Algebra decided he "liked me" and had a girl friend of his call me to let me know. I had gone to the Valentine dance with another guy, Ron, before this call happened. Tim and I had interacted a bit at the dance. So we dated the rest of ninth grade, some of tenth, and then he told me he wanted to invite his friend Helen to the homecoming game. It was nice of him to give me a heads up, but I was crushed. I was invited to the overnight girls' party for Helen that Beth gave. Though I liked Helen, it was still painful and awful for me. I tried acting like everything was fine. Tim and I never went out again.

During my sophomore year in high school, I asked my mom to trim my hair, not realizing she had been drinking. The left side was much shorter than the right side, something that would have been fashionable in the 2000s, but not in the 60s. I would have been aghast at going to school the next day, but had learned with great skill to turn off emotion and pretend everything was just fine. From then on, I went to a professional to have a haircut.

My parents were drinking more and more. Mom worked some nights and Dad would come home from work and get a half gallon of licorice ice cream, and sit and watch the TV for hours. We would all come and go, or sit with him, but his eyes stayed on the TV. If he did say something, it would be a complaint or criticism of Martin Luther King or the march on Washington, and every sentence contained at least one "Goddamn, son of a bitch" in it. Sometimes there was more than one. I recall running an errand with him to pick up some Kleenex at the drug store one weekend. It was January when many stores do inventory, and we found this one was closed. He said, "Goddamn Son of a Bitch, when I get to hell, it will be closed for inventory!"

I started gaining weight, dieting, gaining weight, dieting. Other guys were interested in me, but I was not interested. I still cared for Tim, and still missed Gordon in North Carolina.

Between my sophomore and junior years, Mom said we might move again. So, I didn't try out for anything.

My junior year and senior year (we didn't move) Scorpion stole money from me for drugs and played music loudly enough that I'm surprised the neighbors didn't call the police. I did anything to stay away from home. I had a job and hung out with friends as much as possible.

Finally my brother was sent to a boy's camp in northern Arkansas. Peace at last with the exception of my parents drinking and making loud noises having sex. Note to self, don't choose the bedroom under the parents' room. Not good.

Chapter 11

I chose to stay at home for my freshman year of college. I pledged a sorority, worked, and went to school, so was busy all the time. I didn't know who I was or what I wanted to be, so I chose the math-English track for teaching. All was okay until second semester calculus in which the professor saw no need to explain more than the book offered. My first semester calculus was great and the teacher explained things, so I understood it. Second semester calculus was more complicated. I don't recall hearing about the concept of having a tutor when a subject became challenging. I could have asked for help. It would have made a big difference.

The summer before the senior year of college, my sorority sister Margaret went to the Kappa convention. Since she and I played tennis a lot, she asked if her brother would play tennis with me in her absence. He did, and we became smitten with each other. We married in December right before our twenty-first birthdays. His was January tenth and mine January eleventh. He finished his senior year and I didn't. I thought I'd work a year and revisit my college plan after that. He was headed to Seminary at Southern Methodist University (SMU), and I was grateful to be out of my parents' house, and would figure it out as I went along.

My husband decided before moving to graduate school that we should adopt some cats. I suggested we find out if we could have cats in the dorm. He chose a friend who had been to graduate school to ask, and of course his friend said, "Sure, you can bring cats." So, guess what we learned after listening to cat distress for five hours in the car, and moving everything to the third floor? No, you cannot have cats in the dorms. So, we kept them hidden as much as possible, until the day the female became pregnant, and the birth occurred at seven a.m. one Sunday. Other couples joined us for pancakes and bacon as we awaited the arrival of three Blue Point Siamese babies.

They were precious, but we couldn't keep them and cried for hours as we took them to a vendor who sold them for us. We kept the adults, but had to find a place for them when we moved to Arizona for an internship.

I didn't give myself permission to find more accurate information and relied on someone who just found the answer he wanted. That happened a lot in our marriage—my not speaking up, and spending seven years feeling powerless in the relationship. We may not have lasted seven years had I spoken up, but at least I could have allowed myself more influence.

Once we lived at SMU and I found a job, I gave more thought to a career. I decided to get a degree in recreation, so I could work with children and teens and complement his ministry that way. I didn't play piano, so that was out. So I worked and attended Texas Women's University and finished my undergraduate degree.

It was a good degree, honors and all, and looked nice in its frame. But I really didn't enjoy any of the jobs. Recreation at nursing homes, recreation at churches and camps, are all loving endeavors. They just did not fit the vision I had for myself over the long haul. It was a foreign country to me compared to the world of teaching and counseling that fits me like a calfskin glove now.

The summer of our seventh year, he left for a younger girl. We were twenty-seven years old; she was nineteen years old and adored him in ways I didn't. He also left the church, because the church said his affair wasn't a good fit for it.

Chapter 11

I had lots of cues over the seven years that he may not be happy with me. Every new woman he met, he had a crush on. He would say, "I have a crush on Judy" (or Paula, or Nancy). He would tell me he spent the evening giving Judy a massage at his United Methodist Church national meeting. We went to this meeting in New Orleans to enjoy the historic hotel and city and meet his obligation to attend the meeting. So here we are with all these religious gurus, and he's massaging this eighteen-year-old in her hotel room. He would then excitedly tell me how much he liked her, and that we needed to stop and visit her while driving through California next summer.

When he left, it was shock and not so much awe. He wanted only two things when he left: the car and the waterbed.

Chapter 12

At first I went home to visit family and friends, none of whom knew what to say or do. I naively thought my parents would be transformed from their drunkenness and wrap their arms around me and say, "Oh, honey, we are so sorry to hear he left you. It must be so very hard to even breathe."

Instead my parents got in the pool with their friends and drank martinis until they stumbled back to their place.

Even old boyfriends and girlfriends did not know what to say to me.

Right after he left, the church asked me to start a single adults group. Though I was hardly in shape to run a program, I did it. As a result, I met new friends and stayed busy meeting with the class and planning events with other singles. We square danced, and took river raft trips, and camping trips, and ski trips. I even dated some of the young men. Nobody appealed to me, and some were great guys, like Scotty the choir director who went on to bigger and better churches over time. Scotty was a kind and talented person whom I respected, but I was not ready to love anyone, and barely loved myself.

I spent a year pretending I was okay, and even going on dates, only to return home paralyzed in front of the TV with a big bag of chocolate chip cookies in my lap and crumbs on my face. The tears of sadness of my husband's immediate departure were replaced with resignation, despair, and anything sweet I could put my hands on. As the pounds started adding on, I realized that strategy was not working very well for me.

Cookies tasted great, then I would feel sick and regret eating them; then think I need to do something about this awful habit; then get more cookies. One voice said lose weight and the other voice said, "I don't care, it, I want a damn cookie!" At some point I had to get a root canal too. Thanks a lot, God. After the root canal, which was performed at a dental school, my face was swollen and black and blue for weeks. So, there I was with this puffy face and a body so big only overalls fit. Yes, I gained fifty pounds of delicious chocolate and sugar. Grief sucks.

Chapter 13

It took so much courage to make the call. I had thought about it for several months while binge eating in isolation. But I finally did it. I scheduled an appointment for counseling. Earl at the Pastoral Counseling Center couldn't save me, if I didn't show up.

I tearfully told him about the divorce. He immediately asked me about my family. What did that have to do with my current state of obesity and depression?! It was about the loss, not my messed up family. He gently talked me through the connection of the two and my coping skills. Oh yeah, the TV and food. He helped me grieve my marriage and my growing up experience. He also showed me compassion and kindness and what a respectful relationship looks like and feels like. I was still uncomfortable in my own skin, but I understood why now.

I started teaching Aerobic Dancing and working at another church. I had been working at a restaurant and a YWCA. Aerobic dancing saved me. The music and movement was healing to my spirit. It reconnected me to the days of musical reviews Janet and I performed in her basement for other children on the Army base, and the sounds of Broadway music floating through our house at Ft. Sheridan. Suddenly I was on stage with Nancy singing "All I want is a room somewhere, far away from the cold night air….wouldn't it be loverly."

For the new church I ran programs for the community, and taught Parent Effectiveness Training—*something every human being needs to know*. I wasn't very good leading worship or reading the Bible Verses.

My voice would shake embarrassingly. If I had a song to sing, though, I was good to go.

After a few years at the church, I had a yearning to teach school—something I had dreamed of doing after being in Mr. Dropp's class. I received my teacher certification in math and English and was able to teach at the school of my choosing. This was the early 1980s when math teachers were leaving to work in the business world. The first year was a train wreck. Fortunately the Vice Principal Mary Ann, noticing my ineptness at discipline, suggested the book *Assertive Discipline*. It was the perfect match for my personality. My classroom after that first year was great. We had fun and learned too. Even the teachers who substituted for me bragged about my students' behavior. When I did my student teaching experience in Miss Morgan's seventh grade honors math, discipline was easy. Miss Morgan taught five honors math classes every day. We could laugh a bit, and go back to the task at hand easily. I had a good experience with Miss Morgan's classes, but it did not prepare me for every kind of classroom. Hence the need for Assertive Discipline; my need for social tools to manage multiple personalities in one room.

I taught math during the day and aerobic dance after school. Those were busy, happy years.

Chapter 14

Then the seventh year came. I suddenly dreaded going to work, and I thought I would throw up if I had one more paper to grade or one more student to send to the principal or one more parent to call. I took a sabbatical. During that sabbatical, someone referred a student to me for math tutoring. When his grades went way up, I suddenly had a lot of students coming for tutoring. I found out that I love working with students individually doing tutoring.

For four years I tutored students in math, and let myself be tutored in tennis. My dad always said PE majors were stupid, so I didn't take PE once the requirements were met. But I love movement and competition and wish I could do high school and junior high all over again and be in sports. I would be on the track team, tennis team, try out for drill team, and run for student council.

Tennis was this wonderful adventure in movement and strategy. My coach helped me with both and told me to go play tournaments. I lost all of them in the beginning. Then we would discuss what skills the opponents had that I didn't and what strategies to use when playing doubles. I applied his recommendations, and wow! Suddenly I was winning matches instead of losing and talking with him about it.

For so many years I didn't put myself out there. I stayed hidden and focused on work and whatever relationship I was in at the time.

I have a friend who always encouraged her daughter to try out for things. One year she took her daughter to try out for a part in a TV show being filmed in town. Thousands of mothers showed up that day with their daughters. It didn't matter. The daughter did not get the part, but she learned how to experiment. Later she performed in her honors music group and became a star in her own school community, because she had allowed herself to stretch into something new. I wish I had done the same.

As my tutoring business grew, my tennis experience helped me grow and learn new things about myself. I decided to get a Master's Degree in Counseling. I had thought about this in 1978 because I loved my experience with Earl when he helped me after the divorce. I didn't follow through with the idea at that time. I hadn't been ready. I taught math at a Catholic school for four years while doing graduate work in the evening.

Though my confidence grew while teaching and playing tennis, there was still this empty place and doubt about myself. The doubts minimized while I danced or played tennis, but showed up a lot socially, especially among the women on my tennis team. As my tennis partner and I became more skilled and more acquainted with stronger players in the metroplex, we were presented with an opportunity to join another team.

So we left our team, and joined another. Our decision was met with a lot of hostility and it appeared to be mostly aimed at me, since I was the new person on the team. It took several years before people let it go, and I spent those years avoiding people who judged me, and spending time with those who didn't. But the people pleaser in me suffered interminably and shame attacks were frequent and relentless, like poisonous quills hurled into my skin.

I am among those with this cantankerous creature hovering and waiting to attack.

In a session I had when once again the inner demon reared its head, probably about my supposition that anyone would want to read a book I write, my therapist sent this text to me:

Chapter 14

"Ms. Simmons, I have been thinking about our session. More specifically, I have been thinking about that CRAZY, CRITICAL VOICE from the Gulag. Pam, you are a beautiful, bright, accomplished, kind, compassionate, reliable, responsible, honest, brave and loveable woman. That voice in your head from the work camps of hell, is Barking Mad—full of distortions and lies that are laughable to anyone who knows you! Tell him to take a flying leap into the world of narrow-minded pissants where he belongs and will fit right in. Just sayin'."

Those words meant a lot to me. They are words I have hungered to hear for years, from parents, from grandparents, from aunts, uncles, cousins. No one ever said them to me. Well, I take that back. An ex said it to me, but by then I had lost respect for him, so I discounted it.

Mary's words helped me squash some of the very critical things my mother would say. When I gained some weight in high school, she would say, "If you lose ten pounds, I'll buy you a new wardrobe." If my room got messy from working and going to school and being involved in sorority activities, she would say nothing. But I would come home at ten p.m. from work to find all of my drawers emptied on the floor. Sigh.

Chapter 15

Mom had always been a clothes horse. Even though her dad worked during the depression, he worked for Bell Telephone and made money when many others weren't at the time. He was good at budgeting and saving. Her dad was one of four boys and a baby girl all born on a farm somewhere in Arkansas. All of the brothers saved and invested well. Mom's mother, Bess Dickson King, died right after Mom left for college at Texas Woman's University in Texas. Her mother was a writer and poet who wrote a section for the Little Rock newspapers for many years and had poems published through the Poets Round Table. Her pen name was Eve Adams. I never met my grandmother, so it's hard to know much about her. I have some of her articles and poems. One poem titled "JOY" I had someone calligraphy for me. In the 1990s I attended a funeral for my friend Scott's father. At the funeral the minister recited this poem for us. I was amazed. I wish I had talked with him about it after the service.

JOY

Let me detain this moment,
Let something remain with me of all this rapture.
Oh, that I could capture and hold the fleeting instant.
Wherein life trembles and stands heart-stricken on the high white hill of bliss!
Be swift, my feet, to overtake the fast receding instant.
Be strong, my hands, wrest from this transient ecstasy.
It's sweetness inconceivable,
For now, oh, now, the wild, high moment passes
Irretrievable.

Eve Adams

Mom was the only child her parents had. Her dad was named Durward and he was stoic and smart, but not very relational. When I tried to give him a hug, he would stand stiffly and smile, but not reciprocate at all. He was one of four sons and a daughter of farm folks in Arkansas; all his male siblings and their sister Edith were also stiff and stoic. Having a conversation with these guys was like pulling taffy—sticky and cumbersome and slow. Edith could at least carry on a conversation, but still had a distant persona. When I became engaged to the minister, Granddad showed up at the Sunday school class my fiancé taught. He had told no one he planned to come, so we were both surprised. He had never shown up for anything I did before.

When my dad spoke to Granddad about marrying Mom, Durward sent Dad a letter explaining how much Mom loved to spend money. She bought an entire wardrobe, including a hat for each outfit, for their wedding and subsequent trip to Germany. In every photo I have seen of her, she poses like a model in her clothes. I have a slide of my parents on a ship going overseas. Dad is in uniform smiling as he holds me, and Mom is next to him posing with a tilt of the head in her winter white 1949 straight calf-length skirt, with matching short jacket and hat. Shockingly, there is no monogram on the suit.

Mom had a desire to marry a military man, as she had a lot of respect for them. Her Her college, Texas Woman's University (TWU), had a brother school Texas A&M; and the TWU women loved to get together with the men from A&M. While in college Mom modeled fur coats at Neiman Marcus. I can imagine her standing with a slight lean and somewhat side view, head tilted as she did in every photo I ever saw of her as an adult.

In the military, there are formal events at the Officers Club and other occasions where couples are expected to meet with other officers and their wives. She loved those events. She also tended to be a little flirtatious, which might explain why Dad wanted us to live with his mother when he had to go to Germany for two years. Mom said we could have stayed in Illinois. Part of me wishes we had, since I liked the people and schools. But, I wouldn't have had the opportunity to know Dad's side of the family.

So how this clothes-horse fetish began I'm not sure, but I am sure she wanted us to be dressed well. Hence all the "No daughter of mine is wearing that!" remarks I heard over the years. She had some narcissism and some histrionics too; so parenting did become all about her and how she would be interpreted by our behavior and dress. She dressed my brother well too, but had no control over his behavior.

My dad's parents, Mama and Papa, had barely anything, and Dad provided a home for them and money whenever they needed it. Remember they were raising his son, Flake, from a relationship he had before leaving Rocky Mount. When my parents married they wanted to take the baby with them. My grandparents would not allow it. The baby was attached to them by then, so I can see the validity of their position. My mother believed they didn't want to lose the income they received from Dad. That baby became an unhappy obese adult. He tried living with us a while in around 1965, but he had no work ethic and no motivation to have a job or contribute to the care of the house. Mama must have babied him too much. It was sad to see him with so little drive for anything, except watching TV. The Scorpion at least had a drive to be funny and dangerously adventuresome, stealing things, and harassing people.

A few years ago I saw the movie *Blue Sky* with Jessica Lang and Tommy Lee Jones. This is a story about an Army husband and his wife, an alluring, sensual, histrionic, narcissistic woman. I kept thinking, "Oh my gosh! That's my mother!" Mom didn't go naked in the lake as Lang's character did, but she was flirtatious and sensually dressed for cocktail events. She continued to be a clothes horse even into her eighties. Her friends said on her 80th birthday party, "When she dies, I want her wardrobe." My mother's friends loved her. She was kind to all of them.

After Dad died, my sister lived with Mom for five years to help Mom after two hip surgeries. My sister attended Al-Anon meetings to help her cope with Mom's alcoholism that had escalated immensely after retirement. When Dad was alive, they would sit down to watch Jeopardy, and start their cocktail hour with the largest bottle of vodka available. After Dad died, Mom did it by herself. One night Mom fell walking from the kitchen to the den. My sister watched her slovenly crawl along and said, "I guess you better get on that couch or call 911." Mom somehow heaved her body onto the couch and passed out. The next morning my sister took her to a doctor to check out the injuries. Dr. Smith asked, "How did you fall, Becky?" Mom replied "I don't know." My sister, at least a foot taller, stood behind her and mimicked drinking with her hand to the doctor. Mom received a long lecture about the harm of drinking while on pain killers and other medications, and my sister saw to it that Mom never had another drop.

The most amazing thing about Mom not drinking, was her **not** drinking, but also the personality transformation that occurred as a result. Mom became kind and attentive to us in ways I had forgotten were possible. She started treating us with compassion and respect.

Chapter 15

At my niece's wedding when I entered the room, Mom said, "Oh, I like your hair. It looks great." I almost fell over. I do not recall her ever saying anything except, "What did you do to your hair?" When I explained I had a new cut, she would say, "Well, change it!"

So, I am grateful to have had a couple of years with a kind mom. In December 2010 my sister, who suffered from fibromyalgia and a double knee replacement and other surgeries, told my mom she couldn't take care of her any more. She said, "We need to start looking for a home for you." Dee had been living with her and taking care of her for five years by this time. That night Mom had a panic attack and had to go to the hospital in an ambulance. On the way, she died. I did not get to say good-bye and thank you. In 2004, I had written a letter of appreciation to her, and read it to her when I visited her that year.

Here it is:

Ode To Mom

Though as a family we had rough times and I would love to go back and change some things for us all, I realize that stabilizing events helped create a sense of family for us and I want to take a moment to acknowledge that. So this is a thank you note for things that you did and I find myself doing to make my own home a place of tradition and family time.

I think most of all I appreciate music that we listened to and sang to every day from "Green Door" to "The King and I" to "Charlie Brown." As I look back on those days, they ring of lightness and cheer that we could laugh and sing together. It is hard to recall times when the radio or the record player wasn't playing delighting us with sound and rhythm and words. I brought that to everything I did: jumping rope to "Yellow Bird", putting on musical revues in Janet Taft's basement, performing "All I Want Is a Room Somewhere" with Nancy Nicholson. There was always a song in my head. Even now when I work, I know I am in tune with my spirit when I hear words and melody of a song run through my mind.

Traditions of birthday dinners and Christmas Eve dinners around the dining table were events I treasured. Even when times were chaotic they gave us a sense of constancy that in spite of it all we were still together. Sunday pancakes before church started the day right. Breakfast together at Mama's united us before taking off for school or work. I remember a hamburger dinner when Donnie ate six big hamburgers and we laughed at how thin he was and yet able to put them all away. Sunday "chicken in a basket in the basement" watching Ed Sullivan ended the weekend with union.

The house always looked nice and is to this day a frame of reference for color and style and balance and design. Though I haven't studied design, I have a sense of what feels right in a room from arranging pictures and furniture to flowers and knickknacks.

You created an atmosphere that welcomed us home each day.

I guess the most important ingredient in my daily life growing up is that when I came home from school or wherever I had been, you were home to welcome me. As I write this, I recall now how empty the house felt when you weren't there and how lost we all were when you went to work and couldn't greet us when we got home. Even if I didn't have much to say when I came home, it was comforting knowing you were there when I returned from a day of not only learning school stuff, but from the challenges of learning who I was with peers. You were a presence of comfort that told me I had a place where I was welcome no matter how the day went or what challenges I met.

I can only imagine what all you tolerated and how difficult it was to raise us while moving around so much. Thank you for creating constancy and union in a place called home. I love you.

Pam

Life and Loving and Teachings

When I look at our family genogram or map of generations, I am grateful for people who modeled relationship integrity for me. Even though I wasn't around most of them until later in life, it's nice to know I'm a part of this group. I feel sad for the Mamas and Papas whose lives were limited because someone wasn't present for them. At the same time, I can love them even with their limitations, since it wasn't their fault. Mama made so many chicken and dumplings when we were with her, and maybe that's what she believed love was.

Relationship issues are the one thing that bring people to my office. It can be relationship to self, relationship to children, to spouse, to dating partner, to parents. They may call because they experience anxiety or depression or addiction, but the core of it is a relationship. When healthy bonding doesn't occur in childhood, it affects how people manage life. Emotions follow a bell curve, going up to about a five and coming down to a zero, as the emotions are processed. Those whose parents were present and available, have emotions that follow that curve. Those whose parents were not, have emotions that shoot up to ten in seconds, or flat line at zero. The good news is that these people can be helped and as a result start to feel better and function better in their lives.

When my family decided we wanted a new puppy, Sammy, when our little Sophie was twelve years old, I decided to research how to bring this new puppy into her life. It's a lovely strategy—something I didn't do when we brought Sophie into the life of Murphey, who had passed away two years before we found Sammy.

Let the dogs meet on neutral ground. We chose the yard across the street. Let them sniff each other. Parallel walk them. That was a joke, since Sammy was barely three pounds and a leash an anomaly to him. Then we put Sammy in a crate in the middle of the den, and brought Sophie in to see him. We let them sniff each other some more, then opened the crate to let Sammy out. When we let Sammy out of the crate, Sophie rolled over so her tummy was up, and she let him climb on her tummy and they played. It was nice to witness her welcome him to our club.

Had I not done the research, the moment might have been different for all of us. It takes a lot of information and support to keep a family together and happy. Anger, shame, and criticism don't work. That doesn't mean people never feel those things, but it does mean they don't have to hurl them at those who matter. Screaming and spanking and shaming do not teach children they are loved and that they matter. Neither does ignoring them. How children are attuned makes a big difference in how they manage life as adults.

ATTACHMENT

John Bowlby, a psychologist and researcher, discovered that children acquire an attachment style based on how the parents interacted with them. Bowlby was born in London to an upper middle income family. His parents had the British stiffness common to the culture. He was the fourth of six children and brought up by a nanny who raised the children in a separate section of the house. There were two nursemaids that helped the nanny. He was primarily raised by the nursemaid who acted as a mother figure. As was common at the time, the mother would see the children one hour a day, when she wasn't traveling for months to visit their dad, who was away on business. Later their dad went to war and sent his wife letters. She did not share these letters with the children, who would have benefitted by knowing about Dad. They would have also felt loved if Dad had written letters to them.

When Bowlby was four years old, his nurse maid left the family. This loss of an important mother figure drove his later interest in attachment theory. At ten years old John and his brother were sent to boarding school to protect them from the bombing attacks during the war. Though the decision was made for their safety, it was still a separation from their parents.

These early life experiences drove his interest in how parents bond with their children. He studied psychology with a focus on maladjusted and delinquent children. Due to the war, many children were separated from their families, so he also became interested in the effect of separation on child attachment. Children who were hospitalized for long periods of time with no access to a parent, also had attachment difficulties, including the inability to bond or have empathy. Hospitals today allow parent visits.

Bowlby later studied how children greeted their parents when they came to pick them up from nursery school. He identified three attachment styles as a result of his observations. Some children ran with glee to the parent and hugged him/her. Others turned away as they entered. Others were irritated. He defined the attachments styles as secure, avoidant, or anxious. There are other attachment styles, but these are the basic three.

Secure children are resilient, feel sad at appropriate times, and have positive emotions. When they reach adulthood, they handle stress and relationships well, and have a good attitude when challenges come along.

Avoidant children appear friendly and independent, but are indifferent to parents' absence or return. Parents are unaffectionate or rejecting of the child's signals. As adults, these people have a hard time hearing about others' feelings and have trouble talking about their own. Their spouses will come in for help, because they feel so alone.

Anxious children are easily distressed by Mother's absence and not easily comforted. They will cling or resist or be desperate. They are also distrustful and suspicious, and can lack empathy. Parents are unresponsive or inconsistent, and tend to regard the child as a nuisance. As adults, these people have rocky relationships because of their ambivalence and anxiety.

The bond with parents is a significant factor in a child growing up to be secure or anxious or avoidant. Most parents are not trying to set up negative experiences for their children. Secure parents will have more success with parenting than anxious or avoidant parents.

Because my brother, Scorpion, was in the hospital several days at three years old, and Mom could not stay there with him, it caused a break in the parent-child attachment. He also had brain damage as a result of the meningitis, so he struggled with bad decisions and risky behavior choices his entire life.

These attachment styles show up in adult relationships. When someone comes in to talk about being discouraged about a significant person in their lives, I show them how to more easily relate to this person. I describe the attachment style, and then what they can do to help their partner feel more secure and loved.

Parenting

Not every parent is prepared to parent. Many become pregnant without intention and have different feelings about being pregnant than a mom who is excited about it.

There are a lot of factors that keep parents from being the best parents they can be. Sometimes it's a loss of a spouse or a child. When someone dies, grief can last as long as two years, and when there is an infant to care for, that infant typically will not receive the care that would have been there without the loss. Some parents have a history of abuse or neglect or emotional limitations that keep them from being present with their children in a healthy bonding way.

When Mom told me that my sister was going to Al-Anon to cope, she said it to me with sarcasm, as though there was no reason my sister needed this assistance. How blind Mom was to the effect she had on others.

Another factor affecting how parents parent is the number of children they have. In families with six or more children, parents can be overwhelmed managing all the people in the house. My dad's dad Papa was the second of ten children. Mama was the second of five children. Mom's dad was the second of six children; her mother was the third of four children. This information helps make sense of the limitations they all had. Most people set out with good intentions, even though the results may not be good. At any given moment, most people are doing the best they can.

Children whose parents attune to them by mirroring their facial expressions and responding with comforting words and actions, will find their child growing up more secure. They get along better with peers and adults, solve problems well, and walk through life with less distress. Consistent eye contact with Mom or Dad, and empathy make a big difference in the child's ability to have empathy for others.

RELATIONSHIP SKILLS

It helps when interacting with other people to check out how your words and actions feel to them. Being conscious about others' responses to you, creates a better bond in the relationship. "I notice you have a curious look on your face. Have I said something to offend you?" Or, if you want to provide some negative feedback to someone, it's possible to limit the blow it can have on them by saying, "When I experience you this way, I tell myself that I'm not important to you, and then I feel pretty insignificant. It would be helpful to me if you would look at me and not the TV when I'm speaking to you."

An important strategy that helps people feel better about themselves and keeps relationships positive, is to maintain a five to one ratio of positive interactions to negative ones. John Gottman and his wife researched couples in a lab. They observed both positive and negative interactions that helped them determine whether the couple would still be together in a year. When couples maintained the five to one ratio of positive interactions to negative interactions, they balanced the negative interactions that break the bond of safety. Positive interactions include how they greet each other upon awakening, how they say goodbye as they start their day, how they greet each other upon returning, and how they say goodnight. These four critical moments of the day can cement the relationship in times of hardship or stress. This information has been helpful to many families. Sometimes adults are so busy giving corrections to behavior or complaining, they forget to point out the things they like.

Martin Seligman, who began the field of positive psychology, had researchers go into companies and transcribe every word said in business meetings. They found one third of the companies were flourishing economically, one third were doing okay, and one third were failing. They coded every sentence for positive or negative words, and took a simple ratio of positive to negative statements. The companies with a ratio better than three to one positive to negative statements flourished. If the ratio was above thirteen to one, credibility was lost by the exaggerated expression of positive statements. The meaning of the words diminished.

We can translate that same ratio into families and couples. Maintaining a ratio of at least three to one positive statements to negative statements; generates creativity, growth, and resilience. Anger and shame beget sadness, fear, and disconnection.

When a mother brought her ten-year-old in because he had been depressed for a while, I suggested she implement this ratio as a nightly routine. The first thing people think about or hear upon falling asleep and upon wakening, are integrated in the brain better.

I suggested that each night when tucking her son in, that she ask him to describe three things he felt good about during his day. After each thing he identified, tell him the character strength he has based on his story. For example, if he tells her he helped a student with a basketball shot that day, he exhibits the character strength of kindness and sharing his talents with others. If he tells her he stood up to a bully on behalf of another student, he exhibits the strengths of fairness and leadership. This routine builds a definition of self based on positive attributes, and builds resilience for handling challenges in life.

Within a week of her doing this nightly ritual with him, the boy was no longer depressed, felt better about himself, and was more confident going to school every day.

I also recommend this routine for building resilience in oneself. Doing this ritual every morning upon awakening and every night before falling asleep helps maintain a positive relationship with oneself. After reading my counselor Mary's description of me, I put her words on an index card that I read every morning and every night. Just because Mom didn't know to do it, doesn't mean that feedback from others cannot be helpful. I also acknowledge my love of learning, curiosity, and social intelligence; and my courage to tell this story.

BUILDING CREATIVITY AND PROBLEM SOLVING

Children love to try on different personas. Halloween is a great time to allow them to do it. Our little one at three years old put on his Spider Man costume weeks before Halloween and pretended to fight evil and bad guys every day. At five years old, he was a Ninja Turtle fighting evil and bad guys. Play is such a good time to pretend to be someone or something and allow possibilities to be experienced. If robbed of the opportunity, the behavior is acted out later. It's really okay to pretend to be Dale Evans or Shirley Temple or Super Girl.

It's okay as a parent to validate the experimentation. It's easy for a child to stand up tall when he or she feels loved and attended to by parents. It frees the child's spirit, rather than creating fear of doing something wrong.

One of the most difficult tasks parents have is maintaining their own emotional equilibrium and managing fears that their child will turn out flawed. When I can stay calm as our son is being something or sharing something with me at any age, and I listen and attune to his feelings about what he's being or telling me, he learns how to attune to himself.

When I worked with parents and teens for several years at an agency, I asked the teens what they would most like to have changed in their families. Every time I received the same answer, "Please tell my parents to stop yelling at me." Screaming and yelling are the parents' way of managing their own anxiety. It creates anxiety in the children. So the job as a parent, is to take good care of oneself and one's emotions, so as a parent you can stay calm and attuned to your children.

It's important to nurture and listen to children, before trying to teach them. If their emotions are high, they are not ready to learn. One evening at the dinner table, our son said, "I hate my history teacher." Having been a teacher, my blood pressure started to rise, and a million tacky comments came to mind in response to his remark, like "Don't bad mouth your teacher. Teachers work very hard!" I resisted the temptation to preach and teach. Instead, I said, "Oh, you're pretty unhappy with your teacher today. Is that right?"

He said, "Yes."

"Can you tell me a little more about what happened?"

He said, "Today in class, everybody was talking. But she yelled at me, even though everyone else was talking."

"Oh, dear, I can imagine how frustrating that was for you. I know how you like to cooperate. It must have been embarrassing too."

He said, "Yes, and I'm really mad at her."

"That makes sense. I think I would be embarrassed and angry too."

There was a long pause as we both chewed our food. Then he said, "I think she's kind of a new teacher."

I said, "That's quite intuitive of you. Having been a new teacher once, I recall how hard it was to learn how to keep order in the class. It was very frustrating at first. I appreciate your ability to see the situation from another perspective."

What could have been a battle of opinions, turned into his ability to figure it out on his own, and feel good about himself as a result.

Children are little adults trying to figure life out each day. If they are heard, and their feelings validated, their minds stretch and grow. The prefrontal cortex—the problem-solving part of the brain—is not fully developed until twenty-four to twenty-seven years old. Sometimes people expect their children to think as adults. They will start to think as adults if adults set the stage for considering options for decisions and possible consequences. Using the collaborative model of discussing choices and consequences beforehand builds children's confidence in being able to figure things out. This is especially helpful when children reach their late teens and choices become tougher.

Listening and validating is the secret to helping children. They also benefit from having behavior contracts for them at each age and stage of development. Every new school year, we established a new set of household responsibilities and who would do them and when. The tasks were written down, and a deadline agreed upon, and the document was signed. At the end of the document, we arranged a consequence to fit each task, if the task was not complete.

For example, we said, "We don't want to have to check your room every day and nag about it. Please tell us what day and time each week, you can have your room clean.

"I don't know," he replied. I'm sure he was rolling his eyes in his mind. It took a few minutes of our making suggestions, until we agreed on 5:00 Sundays.

"Okay, great," I said. "I will walk in there on Sundays at 5:00. What is the most important thing you have, that if you would not have access to it, you would remember to have your room clean by this day and time?"

"I don't know, I guess probably my Xbox."

I said, "Okay, great. Here is what clean means. I listed the criteria on paper, so he knew what I would be looking for. "When I walk in your room Sunday at 5:00, if all is clean, then you keep your Xbox. If it's not clean, I will keep it for three days or until your room is clean. Does that seem fair to you?"

He said, "Yeah." Again we're sure he was rolling his eyes, but it worked. Fortunately I never had to take the Xbox.

In fact, sometimes he would get so involved in cleaning his room, he would rearrange it. One day he came running downstairs asking for a yard stick. In a couple of hours, he came running down the stairs again and said, "Come see my room." When I walked in, I saw he had put his trundle bed in the dead center of the room, and his book shelves and dresser and other things around the perimeter. He was so excited. "I can sit here on the bed and see everything!!" His posters were arranged on the slanted ceiling so as he lay in bed, he could see them all.

"Why the yard stick?" I asked.

"So I can measure things to be sure they will fit!"

To this day, he can arrange suitcases in the trunk of a car better than anyone I know.

We also wrote a contract for getting to school. He was in ninth grade at this time, and a bus picked up the students and took them to school. So, since he had an alarm clock and knew how to use it, we talked about what his options were, if for some reason he missed the bus. He considered the pros and cons of walking to school or riding his bike. I offered, "I am an option and can drive to you to school, if you think walking or riding your bike will make you too late. Here's how much I make an hour. Here's how much time it will take me to drive you to school and get back to work. I can take you, and you will need to pay this much."

The day arrived. I saw him race down the stairs and out the front door. A few minutes later, he rushed in the door and threw the money on the coffee table.

"Would you like a ride to school?" I asked.

"Yes."

It was a miserable ten-minute ride to school. I tried to chit chat with him, but he sat with his arms folded, and his chin glued to his chest. I managed my anxiety and stayed quiet, but felt miserable.

That night at dinner, he announced, "You know what I did?"

"No, what did you do?"

He said, "This morning when the alarm went off, I wanted to sleep two more minutes, so I turned it off, since it is right by my bed. That's why I missed the bus. Tonight, I'm going to move the alarm clock to the other side of the room, so when it goes off, I have to get up, and then I won't miss the bus."

"That's a great idea. How creative of you to figure out a solution. I like that," I replied.

Years later when he came home for a visit from college, he went out with some friends one evening. The next morning we were all talking in the den and he said, "I lost my wallet last night."

I said, "That's a bummer. What have you thought about doing?"

He said, "I'll call the restaurant as soon as I can, in case someone turned it in."

"Sounds good. Do you still have a flight back to school tomorrow?"

He said, "Yes. I guess I better find out what alternative identification I can use."

"Good plan.

Children learn when parents set up the opportunities for them to figure out solutions to their dilemmas. Agreements and pre-arranged consequences and follow through on the consequences without shaming and blaming and yelling, sets the stage for their brains to do the work. Then they apply it to other situations, and consider consequences of those choices. The biggest gift we give them is the ability to figure things out. If they can't, then the next biggest gift is information they might need to figure things out. Doing all the thinking for them robs them of developing the part of the brain that does the problem solving.

My parents did not have the educational resources to do all of this. They also had limited emotional resources to manage their anxiety and insecurities. Alcohol was the solution of choice. Alcohol numbs the system and provides a temporary escape, but does not allow attunement and engagement with people. My parents were in the room, but not really available to us. I wanted to do more than that. So, in 1979 I took a parent effectiveness class, volunteered to do telephone counseling where I learned listening skills, and began the journey to learn how to be a better parent and human being. Whether I had children or not, I wanted to be prepared.

If you ask our son, he'll have a very different story to tell about all this. But, the goal was accomplished. Even today, he finds solutions, and takes responsibility. And doesn't blame.

Blaming: The number one avoidant technique for being responsible. When our son was growing up, and something went missing, we would laughingly say, "The dog did it." The truth is, being honest about one's own contribution to whatever negative thing occurred, makes it easier for others to admit their contribution too. He who speaks first, is the most courageous. It is much tougher to own up than to point fingers. I tell this to couples daily. It generates extreme vulnerability to being hurt. But it is good practice for being courageous and loving. Usually the courage and loving is reciprocated. And with the reciprocation is a closer and more intimate relationship.

Chapter 15

CHOOSING A MATE

Another important factor in generating good relationships is choosing a partner for life who is a good fit. It takes eighteen to twenty-four months to really know this other person. The reason it takes this long is that the red flag area of the brain is deactivated due to the emotional rush of early romance. People feel good about the relationship, have their more pleasing personality present, and don't see potential problems; or if they do see them, they ignore them. Many people marry before they have done enough research. Even knowing each other a long time, people can discover they have vast differences about important things.

I was working with a couple once who came because they were fighting about his smoking in the house. As they told me the story, they said they both smoked when dating; but once their baby was born, the wife no longer wanted smoke around the baby. She quit smoking. The husband did not want to quit, and was angry that he had to smoke outside. He said, "I was smoking when we met and when we dated. She knew that about me, and now wants to change me. I'm not willing to change!"

There are a lot of things to find out about. Do you share the same values? Do you require the same things for a relationship? Do you need the same things? Do you want the same things? Values are the higher level topics that are the glue to keep you together. You can differ on what color carpet you want, but if you differ on respect, or cooperation, or smoking, or drinking, or being involved in the same spiritual life, or on whether to have children, then life together will be tougher.

A favorite uncle of mine, Grayson, who was funny and smart and cute, was also a self-professed agnostic. He fell in love with a Catholic woman and they married. He was honorable, so went to mass every week with his family and respected this value his wife had, even though he disagreed. He even took care of her himself when she aged and needed nursing care. After she died, our families were at the Catholic cemetery for the burial. At the end of the service, one of Grayson's adult children asked, "So are you going to become Catholic now, or be buried across the street with the other non-Catholics?" We all laughed at the thought. Many years later, when he went to a nursing home near his oldest daughter, it became apparent he needed to make a decision. His daughter asked again, "Dad, do you want to be buried next to mom?" He said, "Yes." And converted. So, we all got to attend his funeral and burial next to his wife, and tearfully recalled as we stood there, the laughter from years before.

Some people can navigate around higher level value differences well. Others cannot. So it helps to have those tough conversations early to prevent major conflicts later. Conflicts are inevitable and the one thing that allows more stretching and growing in conflict, is the ability to remain calm and dig deeply for ways to make a win-win out of those differences.

MARRIAGE

For decades people married from eighteen years old to twenty-five years old. It's more common now to wait until thirty. Waiting until thirty is not a bad thing. People tend to have better financial status and a better sense of who they are and what their preferences are. So, one's age when choosing a partner matters, and so do preferences and deal breakers and a life vision.

Even if someone marries at thirty or forty, people go through stages of change. That is why having values in common is helpful. It's common for transformations to occur at forty years old or fifty years old. It's hard to know ahead of time, what changes experience and learning will bring. It's important to grow and stretch, and if couples grow and stretch together, it's easier to sustain a long-term marriage.

I know of a couple who married and had children. Mom stayed at home to be available to the children, while Dad worked. After all the children were grown and gone, they sat down together to say,

Chapter 15

"What do we want now?" Dad said, "I want to travel and do things work prevented me from doing." Mom said, "I want to work. I gave up my career for parenting, and though it has been wonderful, I'm ready to work now." They tried to combine the two goals, and in spite of their best efforts, their goals did not coordinate as well as they wished. They mutually agreed to not perceive each other as uncooperative or bad, and instead to see each other as having conflicting values and requirements for their later life.

In these circumstances, some couples compromise and work out a way for both to have the experiences they want and stay together. Some after trying the compromise, mutually agree that their dreams are too different and talk about how to give each other the freedom to allow the dreams to develop.

When I ask couples who come in for help with their relationship, "When did you first notice your relationship start to change?" The answer I hear most often is, "After the first baby was born." The new baby, who is a delight to have, is also an interruption in the flow of time and energy with each other. Some couples navigate the change well, even though it's stressful and beautiful at the same time. It takes a while to adjust to balancing care of baby and care of the couple relationship too. Sometimes when there are two children, Mom may bond with the first, and Dad with the second. In this process the parent child bond can become the primary one, and then the marital bond suffers. It happens slowly and unconsciously. Then one day they realize, the magic is gone. I say this not to scare, but to inform. It's exhausting and joyful to have a baby. It's also challenging to figure out how to love all the kids, and have time and energy for the marriage too.

Greg Baer defines love as "caring about the happiness of another person, without expecting anything in return. It also does not mean, not caring about your own happiness. There is mutuality and reciprocity in love." Anger says to people, "I only love you when you do what I want." Anger can be an emotion used to control others.

It's okay to be angry. It's also important to express anger in a helpful way, not a harmful way. When anger is above a five, on a zero to ten scale, it's a good idea to write about it, yell in a pillow, or beat on a mattress to give it expression. The number one rule about expressing anger, is "no harm to people, property, or animals." It is important to express emotion. If people do not express emotion, it comes out in harmful ways, one of which is harm to the body, since the body holds emotion.

For both couples and families, I recommend regular meetings to address not only things that need to be adjusted, but also to remind each other about appreciations. Once a week or every other week, at dinner or right after dinner, talk as a family about what things have been going well, and what things might need adjusting. Children appreciate having a voice in what happens in the home. Chores can be rotated or adjusted, communication issues can be discussed, as well as a deep check in with how everyone has been feeling about life and family dynamics. Research shows that families that have a regular check in with each other feel better about themselves. Be sure to identify strengths you see in each other as well.

Another helpful thing to do as individuals and as families is an annual assessment of everyone's goals. Life can be divided into about nine or more categories: alone time, family time, spiritual life, community service, physical and mental health, social life, work/school/mission/purpose, hobbies and interests. There can be other categories as well, but it is important to be conscious and intentional about plugging into life at home and away from home. A piece of paper divided into nine sections like a tic tac toe board, is one way to list goals. The center square represents one's alone time.

Please welcome feedback children give you about you. My mother use to say, "If I say black is white, you better leave it that way." She was not willing to acknowledge that I might have some helpful feedback. The purpose of relationships is to help us all become better people. When a child tells an adult, "I notice that you become angry whenever I want help with science." Welcome the information. It's an opportunity to learn something about yourself that you haven't noticed. We all benefit from knowing the good things about ourselves, but also the things that could help us improve.

Getting help is a sign of strength. I recently had a flashback about a counseling session our family had. Yes, it was one session. That one session was fifty long minutes during which **no one said a thing**. No one spoke. If you decide to get help, talk. Talk about everything disturbing to you.

ANGER, TRAUMA, SHAME, AND THE BODY

One symptom that shows up frequently in the body is restless leg syndrome. Much research about RLS indicates that it is a thwarted escape indicator. In other words the legs want to run away from something. Typically that something is a childhood trauma, or several traumas occurring at any age. It's hard to make it through childhood without any trauma. There are so many great therapies available to assist with healing trauma and clearing distress from the body and brain where they are stored.

Many childhood and adult disorders can be diminished, or at the very least lessened, by the experience of unconditional positive regard by someone. That is what attachment is about. Feeling loved and supported by someone significant, which translates into more esteem and more positive regard for others. Sometimes people feel better just by telling a caring person about their lives. A police officer who felt great shame about a mistake he made, shared how relieved he felt when a colleague told him that he had made a similar mistake. Experiencing the validation of someone else's human experience freed him from the emotional prison created by his belief that he was the only flawed man.

We are all flawed, and it's okay to acknowledge and talk about it. Keeping a secret of a moment of shame can disturb every cell of the body and soul, and lead to addiction or early death. A young woman came in feeling the shame of a decision she had made at nineteen years old. Her workmates noticed she was more stressed and irritable, and her boss recommended she find some help. Fortunately her company had a benefit allowing her five sessions with a counselor. We talked about the episode, which helped. But when we decreased the size of the image of the incident in her head, and decreased the emotional upheaval her body had experienced, we also decreased the negative belief she had about herself. She believed she was an awful person to have made the decision, and could not let go of the shame, until she did the work.

Anger is a strong emotion that can poison our spirit and the spirit of those around us. I have a protocol to transform anger, so people feel better, less bitter, and more positive. What I discovered while working with people who want to change their anger, is that as we work together, I hear story after story of moments of sadness and hurt. As we revisit those moments of sadness and hurt, the brain and the body release the emotions. Suddenly the person can breathe more deeply, maintain their emotional equilibrium, and have better relationships. After one week of working with a woman with this protocol, she shared a story with me. At work that day, they had a staff meeting. After the staff meeting, her boss walked into her office and said, "Has something happened to you? I noticed that when Sue said something offensive, you remained calm. I expected you to blow up, but you didn't." This woman said to me that normally she would have blown up during the meeting, but she didn't feel the need.

Loss and life changes bring so many opportunities to stretch and grow. Many times people feel the emotional pain from these changes, and once they have allowed themselves to feel the feelings and talk about them and allow the feelings to settle down, new perspectives and opportunities emerge. Sometimes just talking is not enough.

Some of the therapies of today transform emotions and body tensions faster than just talking. When a man with high levels of anxiety and depression on Monday drops each symptom to almost zero by Friday, it's like magic. He can breathe deeply and think clearly, and function at his job once again. It's lovely to talk. It's lovelier to do something to move levels of disturbance to a manageable level and allow people to breathe and believe in themselves again. My job is a great job helping people be who they want to be with their children, their significant others, their friends, their peers, and most of all with themselves. The relationship to self is so very important. I have the best job of all, and I thank my crazy family for giving me the experiences that led me to it.

Maybe that's what life is about anyway. Living and learning and looking back at experiences with a tear and a smile. Then to be grateful for the people who made the journey what it was, so we learn what we need to learn. At every moment, we are perfect for that moment. The moment is perfect for us. We are not alone. My sister used to say, "I keep marrying the same guy with different colored hair." People fall in love with the familiar. So, she married guys who treated her like my brother did. She has two beautiful daughters, and two granddaughters.

CHOOSING HAPPINESS

Life can be good. I can choose to be grateful for life as it is right now, and let every moment be alive. Even in moments when I want to scratch my head and say, "All right, God. Really?"

Love happens when you shed the masks, and choose to be alive and present, whether the moment is sad, or scary, or hilarious. And if you need help, get some. Thanks to the Positive Psychology movement in my field, we have vast resources for building resilience and life satisfaction, decreasing depression, increasing gratitude, and recognizing strengths in others and ourselves.

I was working with an adult woman who had begun feeling helpless taking care of her elderly mother. The mother lived with her due to her not managing money well and some physical limitations. Through living in the same home, tensions were high for both of them. The mother felt guilty having to be a burden, and the daughter felt hopeless that her mother would ever be happy. The mother was also an introvert and would not take advantage of opportunities to be around other people her age who could enrich her life and offer play time. After listening to them both in a session, I moved close to the mother, and said to her, "Your daughter really wants you to be happy. It's not her job to make you happy. It's your job to decide to be happy. You are responsible for your own happiness. Every day that you decide to be happy makes your family's home more joyful and pleasant. I'd like you to consider getting up every day and choosing to be happy, because you love your daughter, and because her happiness matters to you. And every day make a list of the things for which you feel grateful. And every day let those around you know how grateful you are for them."

Every moment we can choose how to feel. A negative emotion can rise, we can notice and acknowledge it, and we can choose what we want to feel. One year a colleague's house was demolished by a tornado. As the family stood on the street and observed the destruction, the dad said, "There goes our chance for the yard of the month club." They all started to laugh, and then cry, and then laugh again.

One way to develop more confidence and love of self is to offer those things to others. Offering what we want to others, creates an energy that serves us. The gift we give comes back to us more strongly than it was given. It doesn't necessarily come back to us from the person to whom we gave it. The act of giving it, creates it in us.

Before giving advice, or moving into someone's space, it helps to check in first. "Is it okay if I offer a suggestion about this?" "Is it okay if I sit here next to you?" Everyone has a physical and emotional boundary. It can be called a hula hoop. If I'm going to get in your hula hoop, I need your permission. In a marriage there are two hula hoops that overlap, but they are not concentric. The overlap space is where couples negotiate until they can make a win-win around their decisions. The rest of the space in the hula hoop belongs to the individual.

I was working with a couple who came in for marriage help. There were two love seats, and they chose to sit on the same one. However, the wife appeared to sit as close to her end as she could get. The husband started telling me why they were there.

The wife said, "We aren't close any more and no matter what I say, he explains himself over and over."

After she said that, he started explaining himself over and over.

After several rounds, I said, "I can't help but notice you seem to have a strong need to be right. And one thing I know about couples is that, they need to find a way for both to be right. You can be right, or you can be married."

He went on to explain more about his stand.

I interrupted and said to her, "Is this the way it goes all the time?"

She said, "Yes. I want to talk to him about a challenge I have, and instead of listening, he lectures me. Then I don't want to talk anymore."

Once again he started explaining his position to me. I interrupted and said, "You need to stop talking. Would you mind turning to your wife and saying to her, 'I am so sorry I have not stopped to really listen to you. You must have been waiting for me to do this a very long time.'"

He repeated after me, then she said, "Yes. I can figure things out myself. I don't need solutions, I just need to say some things out loud, and have you validate me."

Then he turned and explained himself to me again.

I said, "I appreciate how important it is for you to convince me of your wisdom. You have much wisdom. So does your wife. She will feel better about herself if you let her talk and figure things out for herself. And then, she will love you for doing it. And you will have more sex. Otherwise she will be angry with you for usurping her wisdom. Which do you prefer?"

This is a classic example of getting into someone else's hula hoop. Say, "I have a suggestion, would you like to hear it?" In this case, she probably would have said, "You know, I really don't want suggestions as much as I want to talk it through, so I can figure it out on my own."

I have some friends who are masterful about this. One will say, "Can I interrupt and add some more information?" The other will say, "Yes, may I finish first?" Or she will say, "Yes, I would welcome some more information."

Sometimes in our attempts to be helpful, we rob others of the joy of figuring things out for themselves.

When people feel loved, they are happier and more grounded and more engaged with life.

WATCH YOUR WORDS

Try to start sentences with "When I…" rather than "You…" This takes the sting of criticism away, so people feel open to hearing your story and what you need. We grow from hearing how others perceive us. There are abusers, though, who will beat you up with complaints and criticism. That's not what I'm talking about here. There is a difference in respectful feedback about behavior, and abusive terrorizing. Every day we have the opportunity to learn to be a better person. That is what relationships are about. Be open. Be compassionate. There is also a difference in being open and compassionate, and being a people pleaser. People pleasers forgo their own wishes and desires for others, the goal of which is to be liked or loved. After a while they become angry when people take advantage of them for their kindness; then they feel guilty for getting angry and return to their compensatory behavior. As a result they feel anxious, instead of grounded in reciprocal and mutual relationships.

I treat my poodle with love and adoration and boundaries. Then he does the same for me. It's a treat to feel loved. My hope for you is lots of love, and lots of learning as you go. Dog love is unconditional. Our love can be unconditional, too, with lots of conversation and listening about what works and what doesn't work for each person.

Pam

EPILOGUE

My wife Lynn and I met playing doubles tennis. At first we were on different teams, but later some of my team joined her team. The first time the team captain put us together for a doubles match, we clicked. Her deadly topspin and my well-placed drop shots made the opponents run a lot. There is nothing like team sports to develop relationships. Strategizing, planning, winning, losing, recovering, are bonding experiences. We had no idea how bonded we would become the first time they put us together. We played tournaments with the goal to become ranked in the state in women's doubles. We were delighted to read that we were number one in women's doubles that year.

We had a lot of fun, and found ourselves feeling appreciation, adoration, respect, chemistry, sensuality.

Many years later we moved in together, and the first thing we wanted to do was get a poodle. She had a poodle growing up and my family had multiple poodles over the years. Sometimes I was envious at how much Mom adored those poodles. I would like to have felt that adored too. There is something about puppies. They adore you back, no matter what. It is the best unconditional love around. It heals a lot of wounds when they snuggle up, and run and play, and kiss you with such gratitude, you want to squeeze them like a Teddy Bear.

First we found Murphey, a precious four-pound toy poodle. As soon as we found him, Lynn wanted another poodle, Louie, a standard poodle. We learned we really need to train larger dogs, since they can reach anything. One Sunday after preparing a pound of bacon for a quiche, I walked away from the kitchen for less than a minute. When I returned, Louie had swallowed the pound of bacon with one swoop of his tongue. We put ham in the quiche instead.

In his third year, Louie developed Addison's disease, and died. Addison's is the same disease President Kennedy had.

We moved into a lovely new area surrounded by creeks and trees and great neighbors. We planted a tree in a spot visible to the kitchen table, and called it the Louie tree. We could talk about Louie and recall all the funny stories of his antics. Eventually we wanted another poodle; one that would play with Colin, Lynn's nine-year-old son. Murphey was so small and a little intimidated by Colin's little boy constant movement. So, we all went together to pick out Sophie, a precious chocolate-mink-colored poodle. She had an amazing spirit and played with Colin nonstop, running up and down stairs and letting him dress her in all kinds of crazy garb. When he went away to college, she was forlorn. We could tell, because when he came home to visit; he would pick her up and she would look adoringly at his face, and appeared as though she was in heaven.

While Colin was still in college, little Murphey's kidneys gave up. Our vet came over to check on him, and let us know it was time for Murphey to go. We left Sophie at home, as we rushed out the door to go to the vet's office, so she could put him to rest. We cried all the way home and for a month after that. We were so sad, we didn't notice that Sophie had not picked up and toy in about a month. One day, we noticed her tossing her ball and chasing it, and realized she had been feeling the same way we had.

Last May, when she was sixteen years old, she died. The night before, when going to bed, little Sammy gave her a kiss. He knew she wasn't well. We knew she was probably ready to go. We called Colin, and the next morning we all went together to the vet. We wanted to say our goodbyes together and let her know how much we loved her. Then we cried and cried and cried.

Little Sammy is four years old and four pounds and loves to work with me. Many clients breathe a sigh of relief the first time they enter my door, and discover Sammy waiting to greet them. He is quite an ice breaker. At this moment he is in my lap as I write.

Colin occasionally does stand-up comedy, and tells stories about us. He's still figuring out his professional path as many twenty-five to thirty-year-olds do. We both remind him that we had several different jobs until we discovered the perfect one.

Lynn retired from her sales job with Thomson Reuters a few years ago, and is happily doing lots of volunteer work, and bringing in extra money working at a desk. Every day she is grateful to not have a quota, and smiles a huge smile.

I continue seeing clients in our living room five days a week with Sammy's help. Lynn and I both value staying in shape. She is a very fast swimmer and she and her team set records at swim meets. I prefer Jackie Sorenson's Aerobic dance for the music and choreography. It is my therapy and I love every minute of it. I also do hot yoga to help repair the physical damage dance can do. Life has been good and we are grateful for so many blessings and so many people who care.

Unconditional love cures heartache, pain, disease, sadness, depression, anxiety, and low self-esteem. My colleague Greg Baer has a book that talks about how real love eliminates every condition in the Diagnostic and Statistical Manual of Mental Disorders. As a society, we have a lot to learn about parenting, marital relationships, and business relationships. The world would be a better place if we all took the time to learn how to love. There are an abundance of resources available to people now. I decided in 1978 that I wanted to be prepared to parent. So, I signed up for the course called Parent Effectiveness Training I told you about earlier. I took it. I trained to teach it. I taught it. I used it. I still use it. It is one of the best things I ever signed up to do.

ABOUT THE AUTHOR

Pamela Simmons is a licensed professional counselor and supervisor of counselor interns in Texas. She has tried on many hats. She has been a church program director, a camp counselor and recreation leader, a sales clerk, a math teacher, a math tutor, and now a counselor. She has had a column in three local papers with more articles than she can count. She presents on Authentic Happiness and Building Lives of Joy.

As a writer, columnist, teacher, counselor, coach, and workshop and seminar leader, she enhances her work with humor and humanness. She guides you toward the love and joy you are designed to have in your life. Her life and executive coaching program is a respected and recognized one for participants who would like to meet by phone from anywhere in the United States.

www.joyfulrelationship.us

Acknowledgments

To my precious wife, Lynn, who has tolerated my dedication to writing this, and supported me through the ups and downs of doing it. To our son, Colin, without whom I wouldn't have learned to be a better parent, or have examples to give.

To my biological family who gave me the material to write about.

And to my writing coach, Donna Kozik, whose patience and encouragement and occasional slap on the butt, kept me going with laughter and tears.

To my beautiful poodles who brought such joy into my life: Murphey, Louie, Sophie, and Sammy. Murphey, Louie, and Sophie are in poodle heaven. Sammy is still here loving us.

To all the lovely people I have met over the years who taught me, tolerated me, and tested me.

If you want to feel better about yourself and your relationships, contact me via my website

www.joyfulrelationship.us

Come to my website and find ten tips for more confidence.

Made in the USA
Lexington, KY
18 January 2018